COLOR TEST PAGE

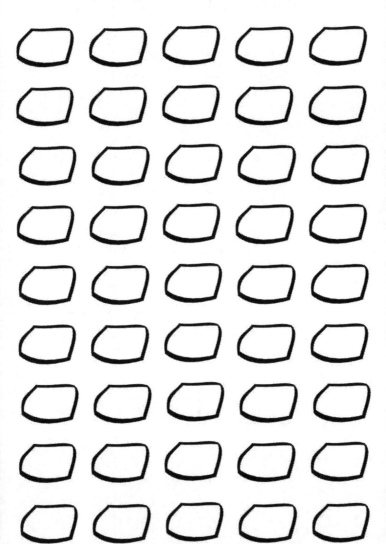

¡¡ FELIZ NAVIDAD !!

TYRANNOSAURUS REX

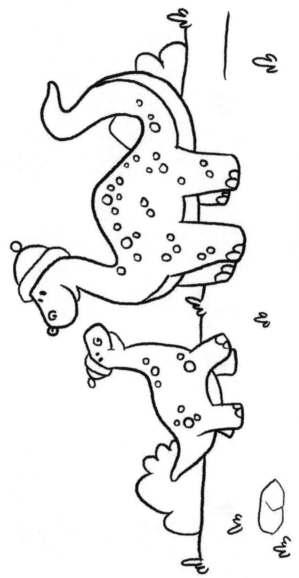

¡¡ JOYEUX NOËL !!

RIOJASAURUS

¡¡ FELIZ NATAL !!

TRICERATOPS

ii BUONE FESTE NATALIZIE !!

DIPLODOCUS

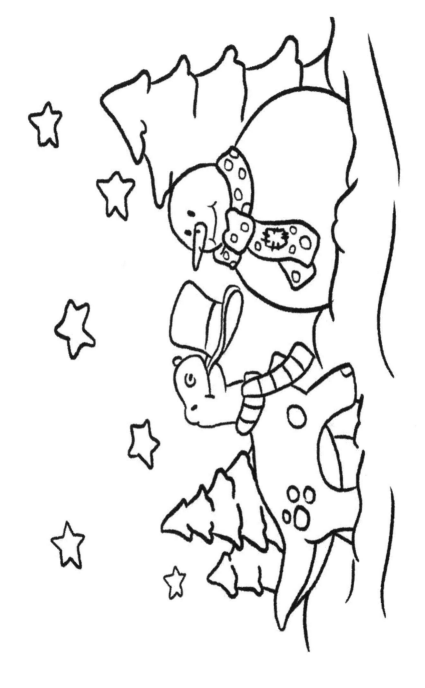

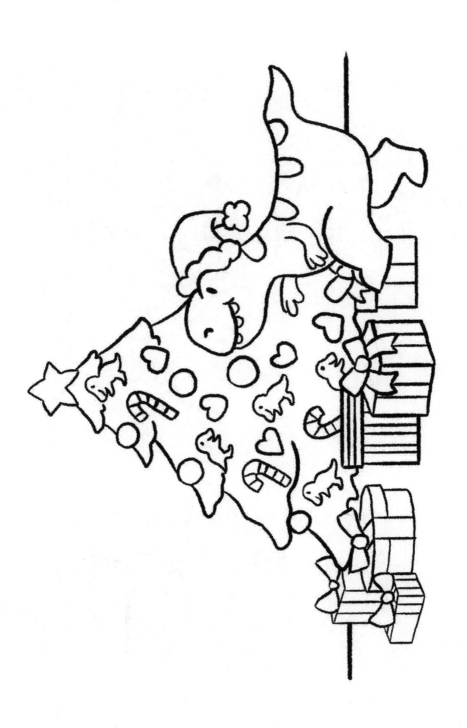

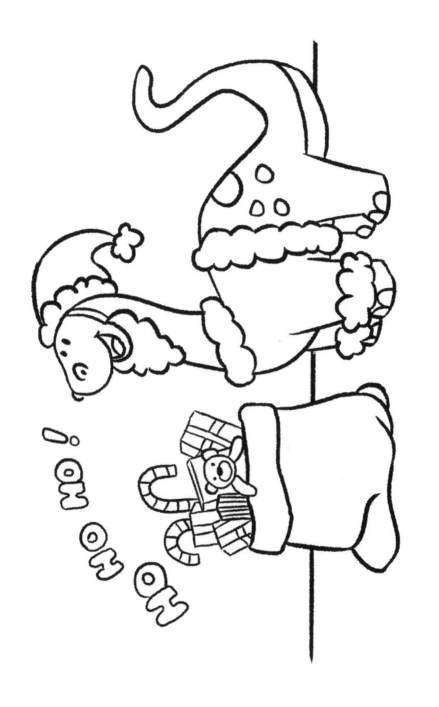

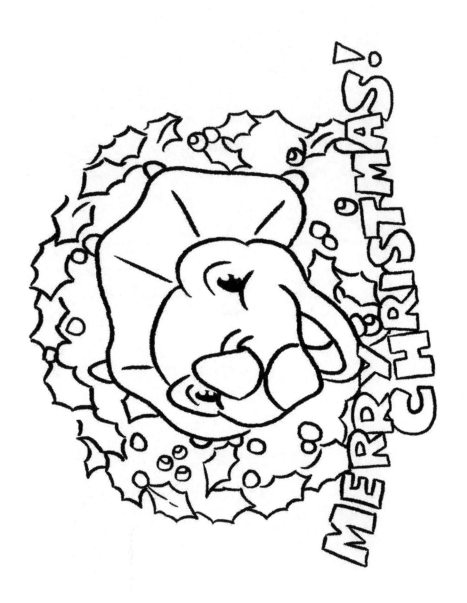

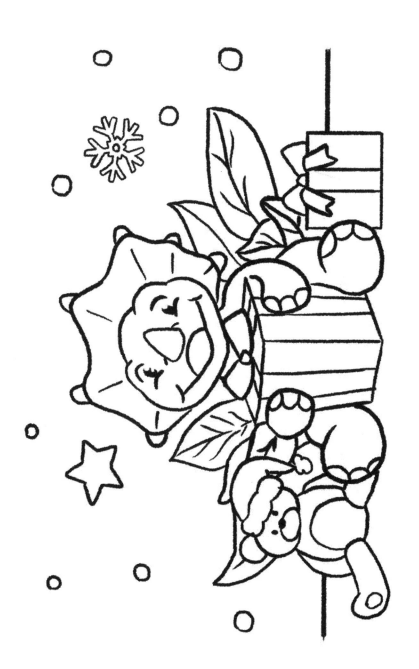

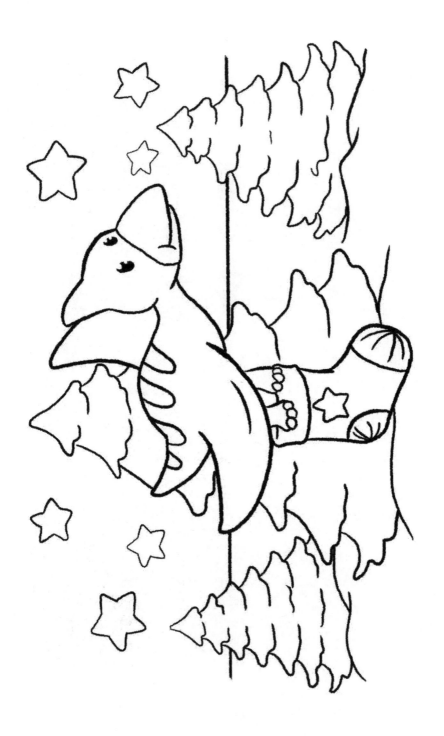

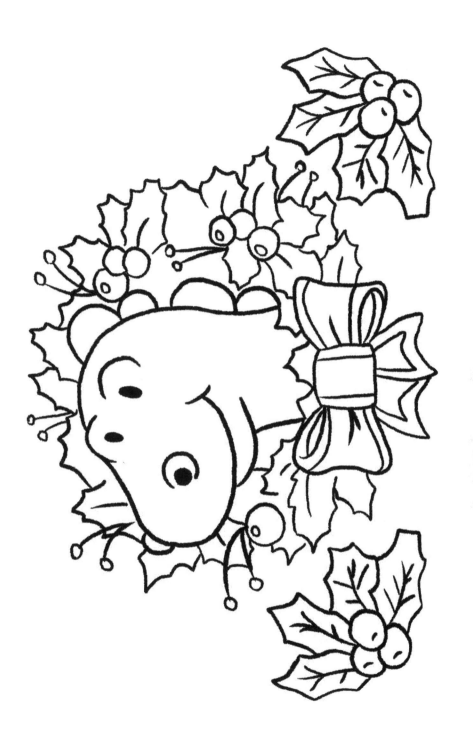

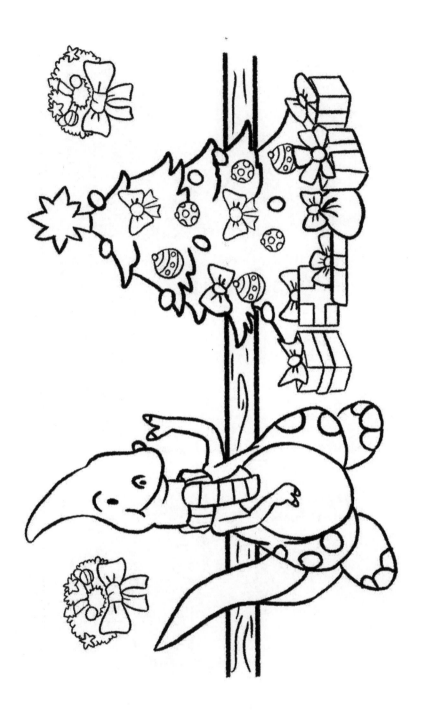

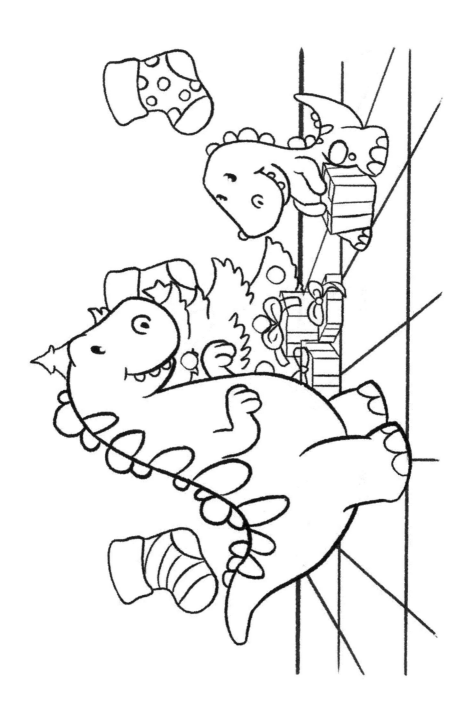

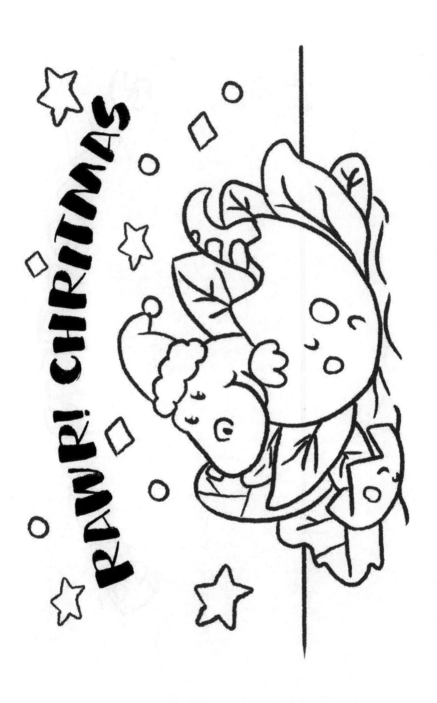

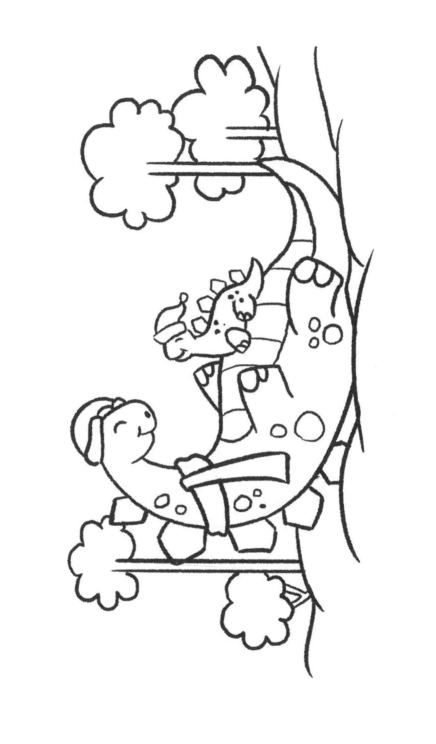

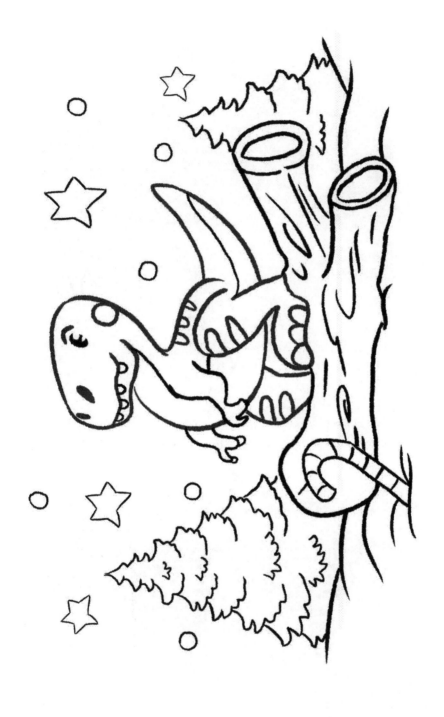

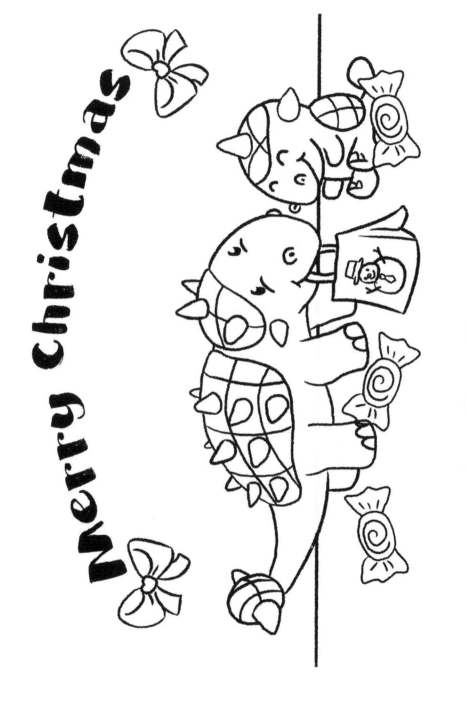

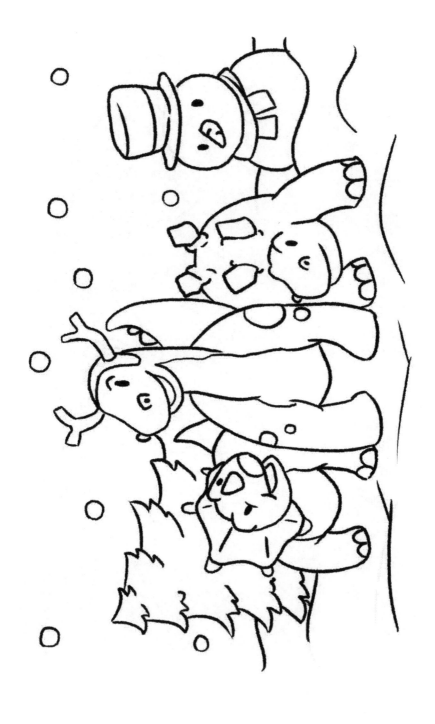

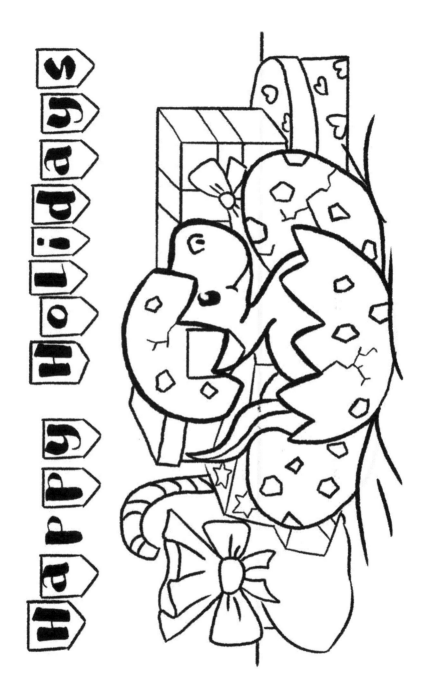

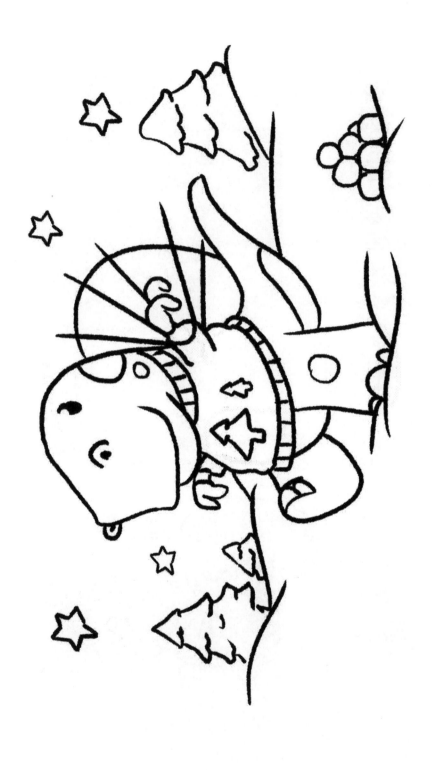

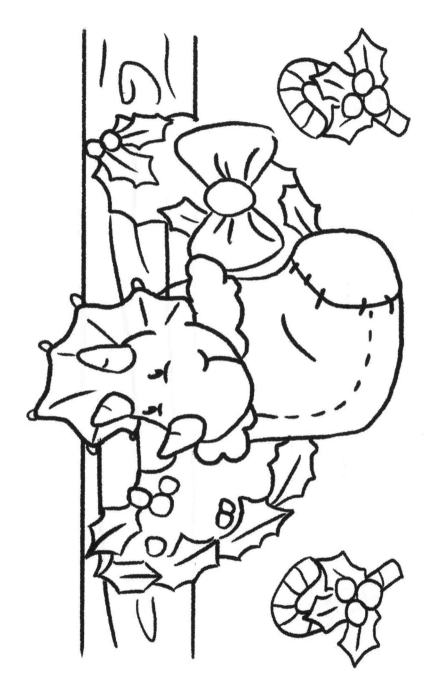

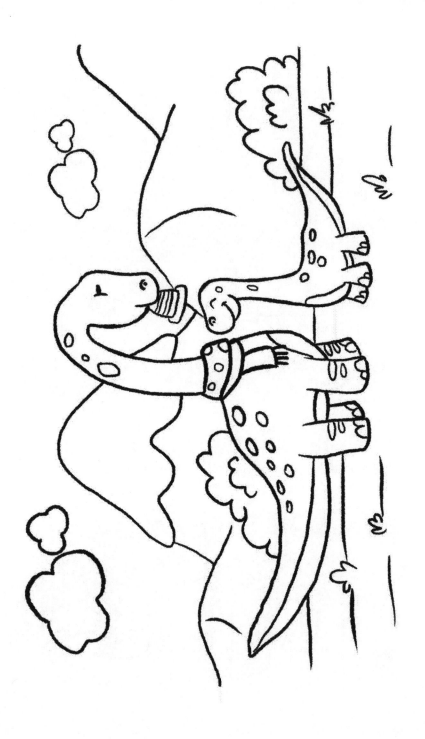

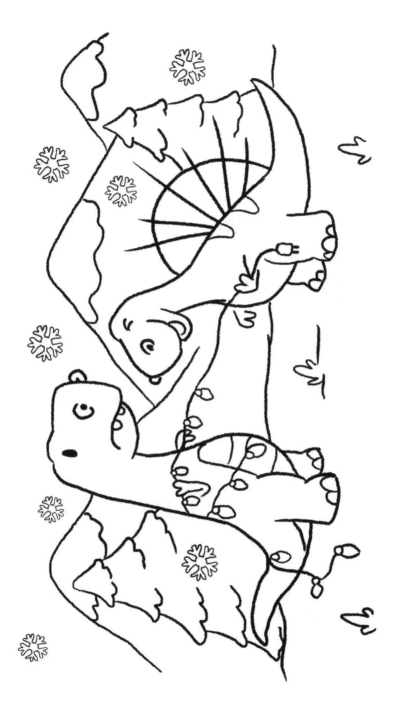

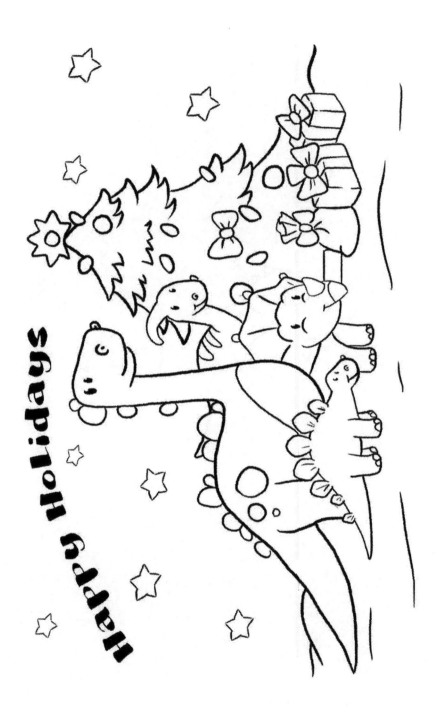

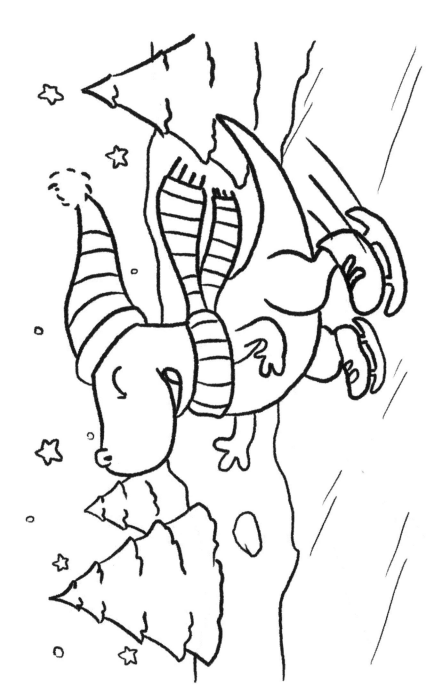

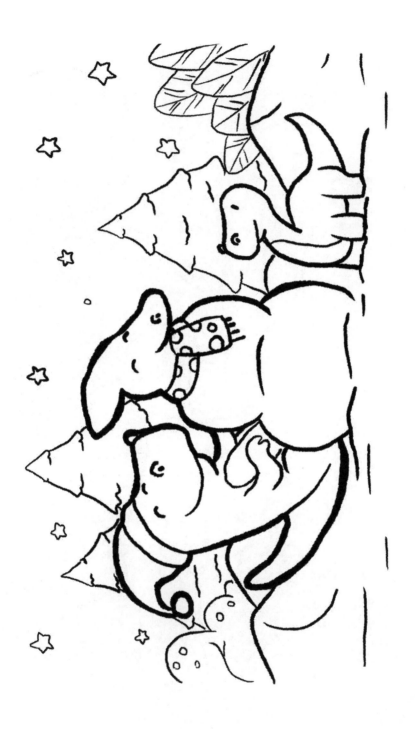

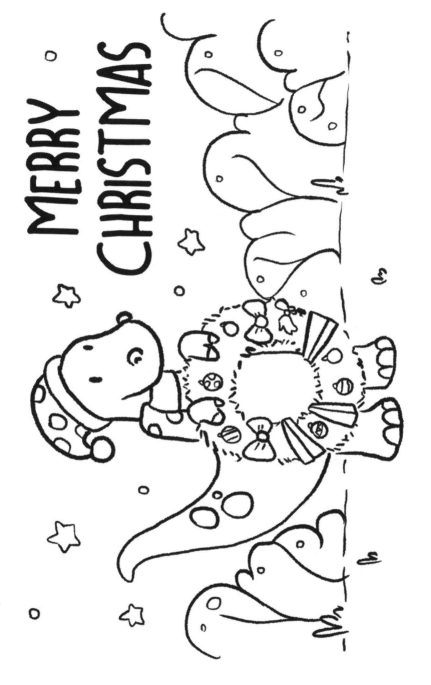

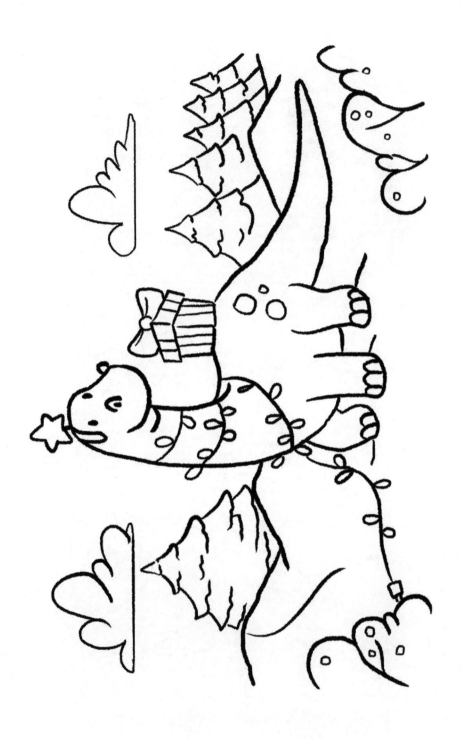

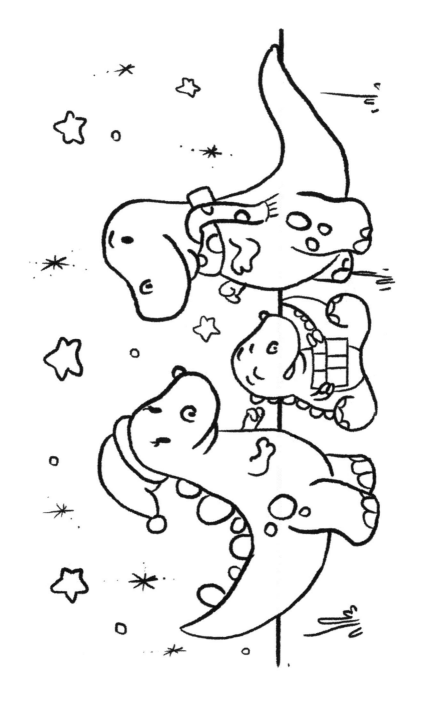

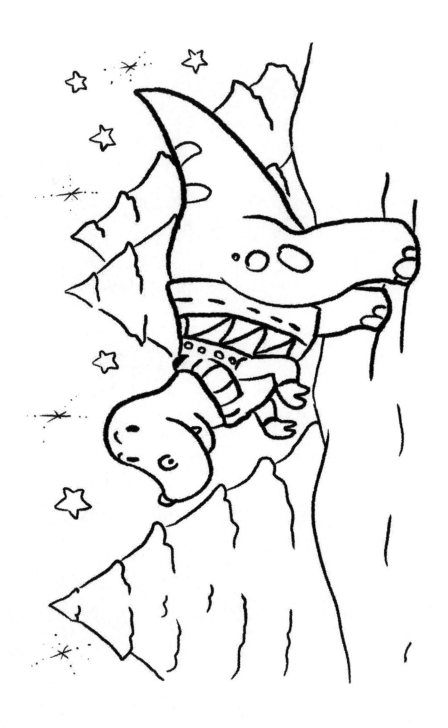

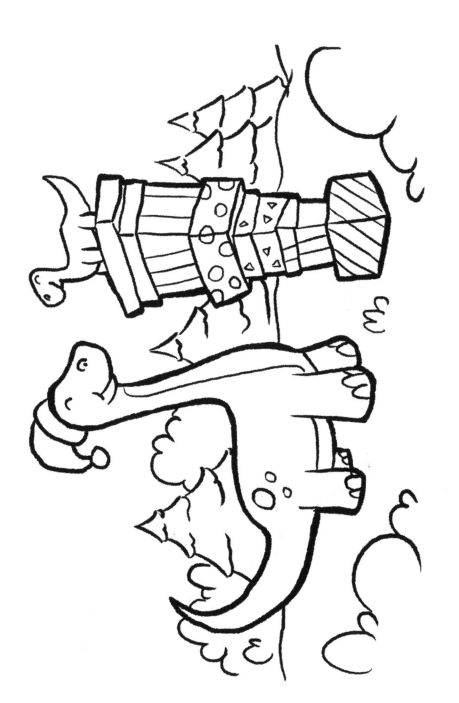

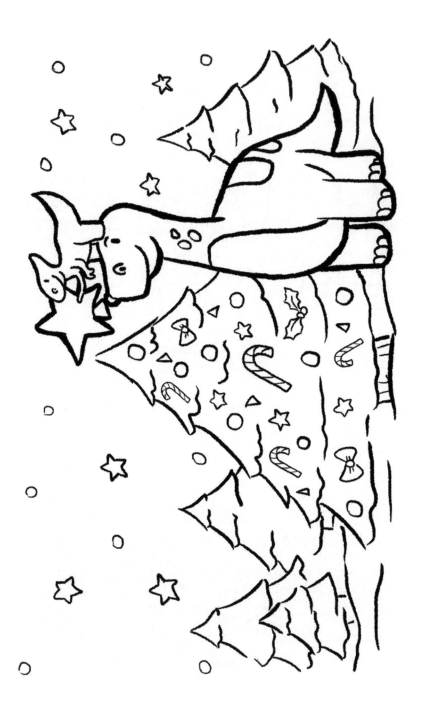

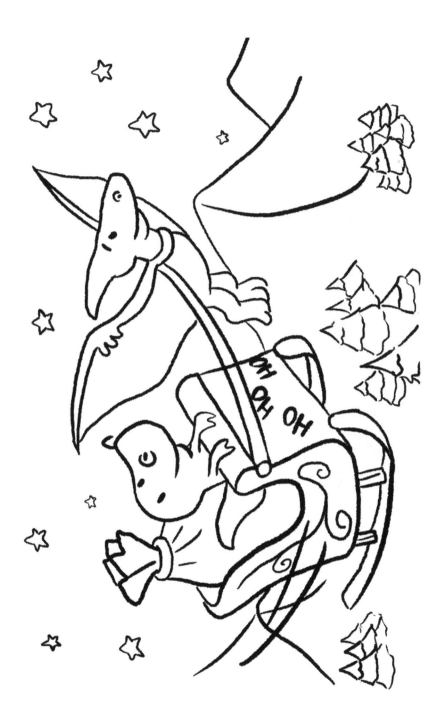

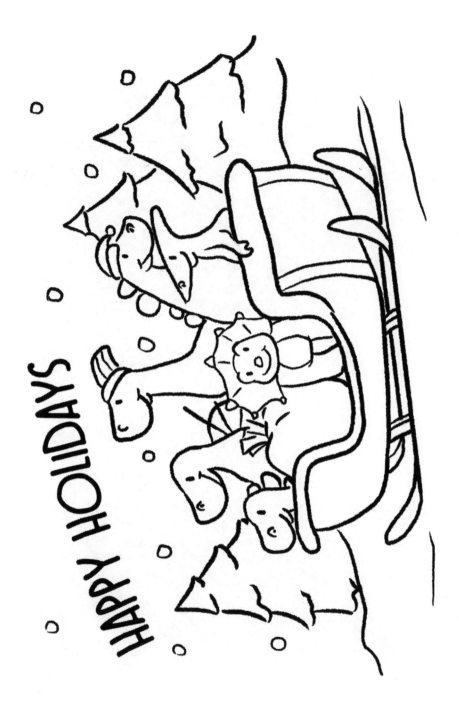

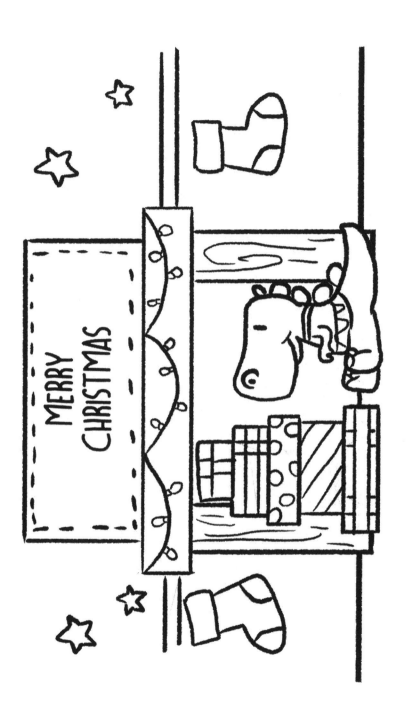

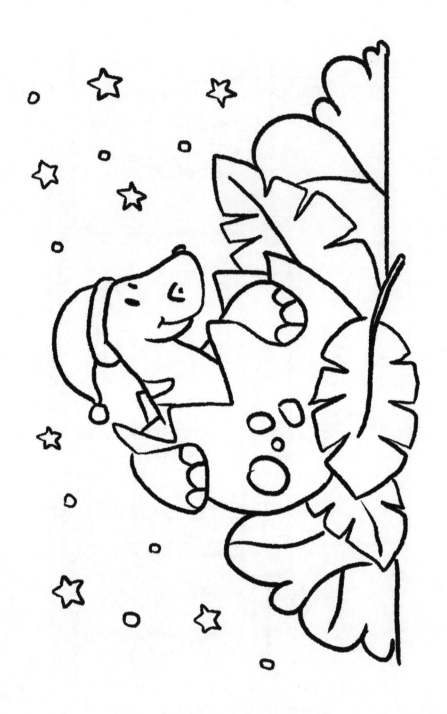

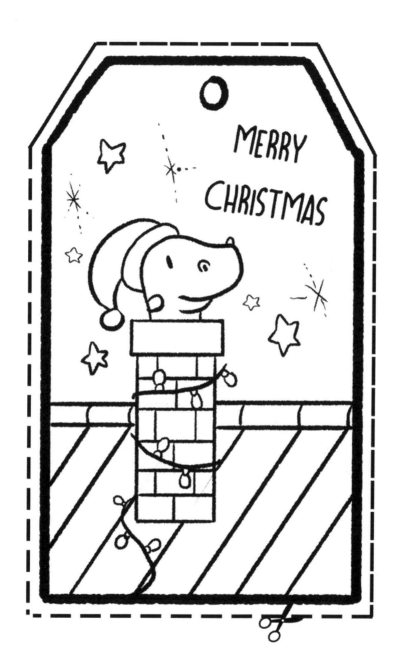

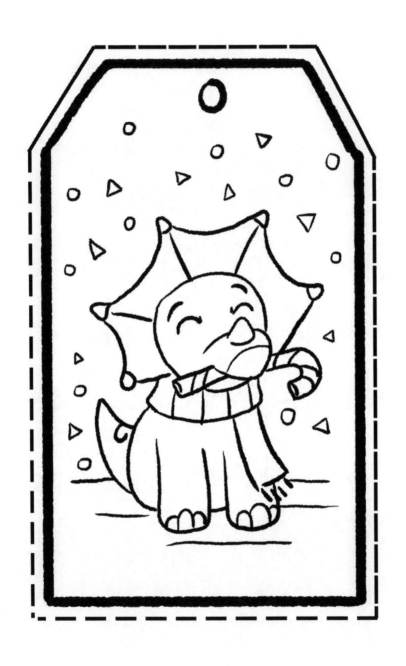

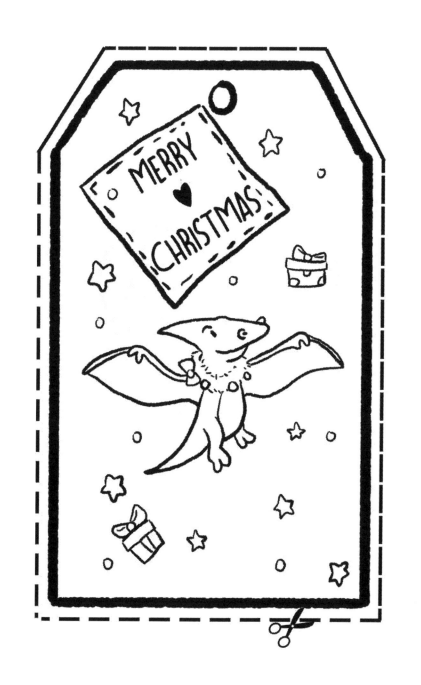

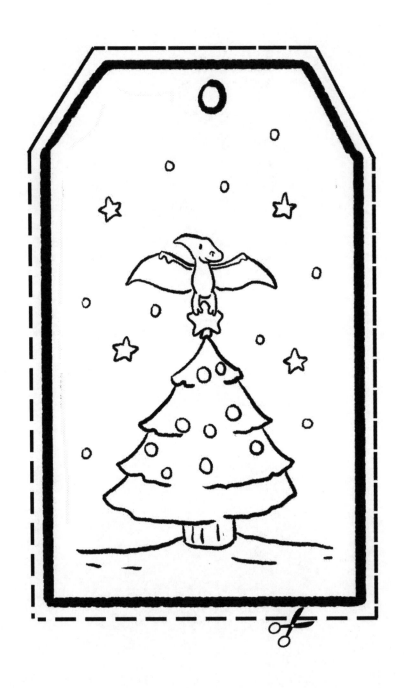

Made in the USA
Middletown, DE
01 December 2019

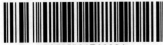